<u>Introduction to *(This)*</u>

In a world that often encourages conformity, we sometimes forget the beauty and power of our differences. This book, *(This),* is a celebration of individuality—a collection of quotes that remind us that we are not the same, and that's what makes each of us unique.

Within these pages, you'll find reflections that challenge the notion of sameness and invite you to embrace your own identity. Each quote serves as a reminder that our diverse experiences, perspectives, and backgrounds shape who we are. It's an invitation to appreciate the richness of our differences, to connect with others on a deeper level, and to recognize the strength that comes from being authentically ourselves.

May these words inspire you to celebrate your individuality and honor the uniqueness of those around you. Remember, it's our differences that create a vibrant tapestry of human experience—let's cherish that

Author: Ordelia Jooste

Table of Contents

Ordelia Jooste

<u>**Themes for Initial Quotes:**</u>

1. **Identity**: Explore the concept of personal identity and how each person's journey is unique.

   "Our stories are not identical; they are what make us who we are."

2. **Perspective**: Emphasize how different viewpoints enrich our understanding of the world.

   "Two minds can never see the same view; it's in our differences that we find depth."

3. **Acceptance**: Highlights the importance of accepting and valuing differences.

   "To be different is to be human; it's our uniqueness that we should embrace."

4. **Individual Experience**: Focuses on the significance of personal experiences in shaping identity.

   "Every path is distinct, shaped by our choices and experiences."

5. **Strength in Diversity**: Celebrates how diversity can lead to strength and innovation.

   "Like colours in a painting, our differences create a masterpiece."

Ordelia Jooste

We Are Not the Same….

"We are not the same, and that is our greatest strength."

"In a world of mirrors, be the one that reflects your true self."

"Your journey is yours alone; cherish the steps that set you apart."

"Embrace the contrasts; they are what paint life with vibrancy."

"Different paths lead to the same destination: understanding."

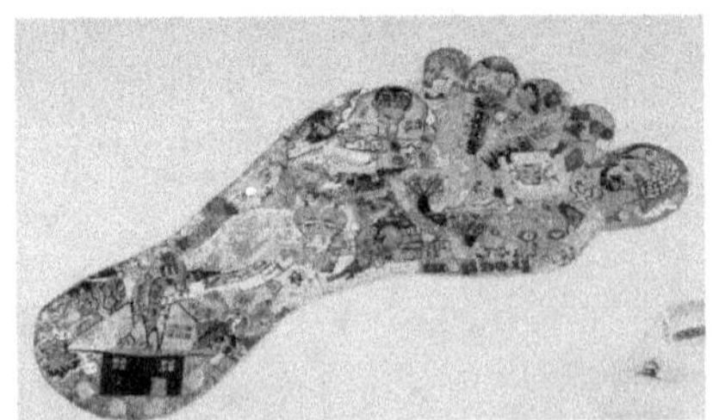

Ordelia Jooste

We Are Not the Same….

"Our paths diverge, yet our journeys inspire."

"In diversity, we find our true strength."

"Uniqueness is not a flaw; it's our greatest asset."

"Different stories make for a richer narrative."

"Embrace individuality; it's the spice of life."

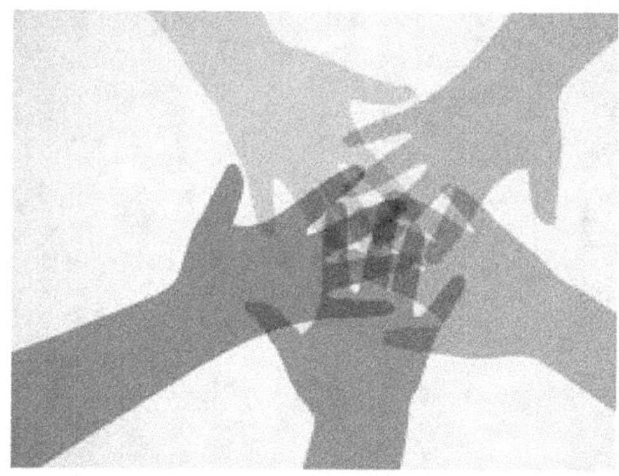

Ordelia Jooste

We Are Not the Same….

"We may not mirror each other, but we reflect humanity."

"Variety is the canvas of existence."

"Our differences are the colours that paint the world."

"In a sea of sameness, stand out like a beacon."

"Each voice adds depth to the symphony of life."

Ordelia Jooste

We Are Not the Same….

"Unity thrives in the embrace of diversity."

"We are threads in a tapestry, each unique yet connected."

"Celebrate what makes us different; it's what makes us whole."

"In contrast lies the beauty of understanding."

"Together, yet apart, we create a vibrant mosaic."

Ordelia Jooste

"What resonates with you the most?"

Empathy…

"To empathize is to see the world through another's eyes; our differences become bridges, not barriers."

"In the heart of every story lies a unique experience waiting to be understood."

"Empathy invites us to walk alongside others, recognizing that every journey is worthy of respect."

"When we listen with empathy, we honor the richness of each person's narrative."

"Understanding begins where judgment ends; embrace the stories that shape us."

Ordelia Jooste

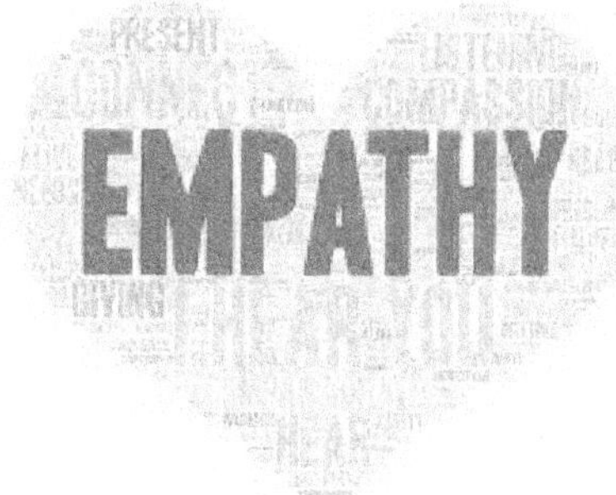

Empathy…

"Empathy bridges the gap between hearts."

"To understand is to connect; to connect is to heal."

"Listening with compassion is the first step to understanding."

"In another's shoes, we find our shared humanity."

"Empathy transforms understanding into action."

Ordelia Jooste

Empathy…

"A single act of kindness can ripple through the soul."

"Feeling with others is the essence of being human."

"Empathy is the language of the heart."

"Compassion is the antidote to isolation."

"In empathy, we discover the power of vulnerability."

Ordelia Jooste

Empathy…

"True strength lies in our ability to empathize."

"Every story deserves to be heard with an open heart."

"Empathy lights the path to deeper connections."

"To empathize is to step into the light of another's experience."

"With empathy, we can transform judgment into understanding."

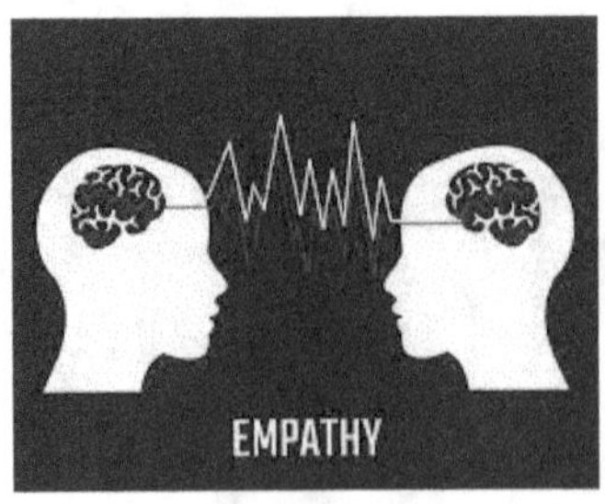

Ordelia Jooste

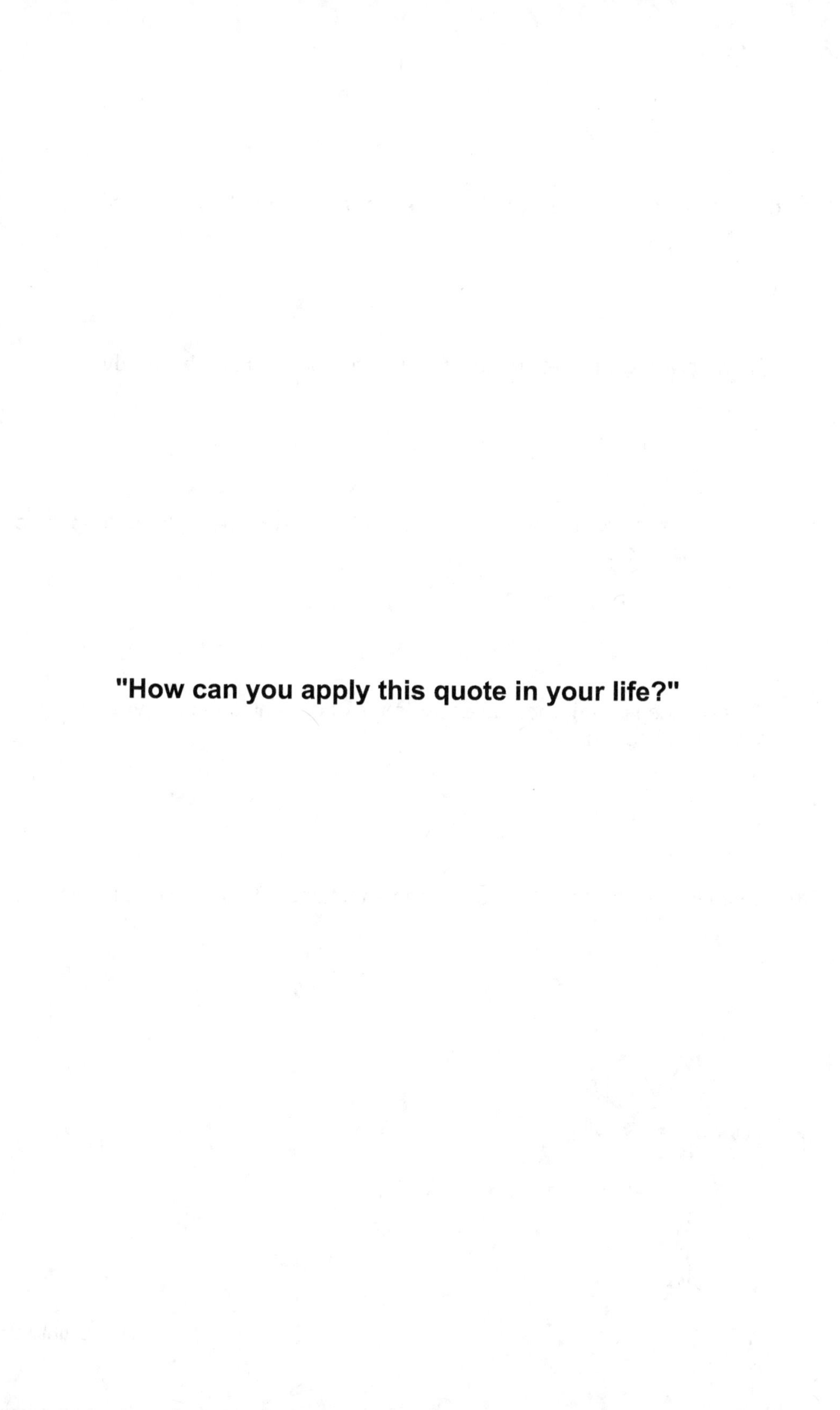
"How can you apply this quote in your life?"

Resilience…

"Our differences are the roots of our resilience; they ground us when storms arise."

"In embracing who we are, we find the courage to rise above adversity."

"Each challenge met with authenticity strengthens the foundation of our character."

"Resilience is born from the acceptance of our unique journeys, turning struggles into triumphs."

"Our scars tell stories of survival; each one a testament to our unique resilience."

Ordelia Jooste

Resilience…

"Resilience is the strength to rise after every fall."

"In the face of adversity, we discover our true power."

"Every setback is a setup for a comeback."

"Resilience turns obstacles into stepping stones."

Ordelia Jooste

Resilience…

Resilience is not about avoiding the storm, but about learning how to dance in the rain."

"The human capacity for burden is like bamboo—far more flexible than you'd ever believe at first glance."

"It's not whether you get knocked down, it's whether you get up."

"Out of difficulties grow miracles."

"When everything seems to be going against you, remember that the airplane takes off against the wind, not with it."

Ordelia Jooste

Resilience…

"You may have to fight a battle more than once to win it."

"The world breaks everyone, and afterward, some are strong at the broken places."

"Do not judge me by my success, judge me by how many times I fell down and got back up again."

"Hard times may have held you down, but they also made you stronger. Now stand tall and embrace your strength."

Ordelia Jooste

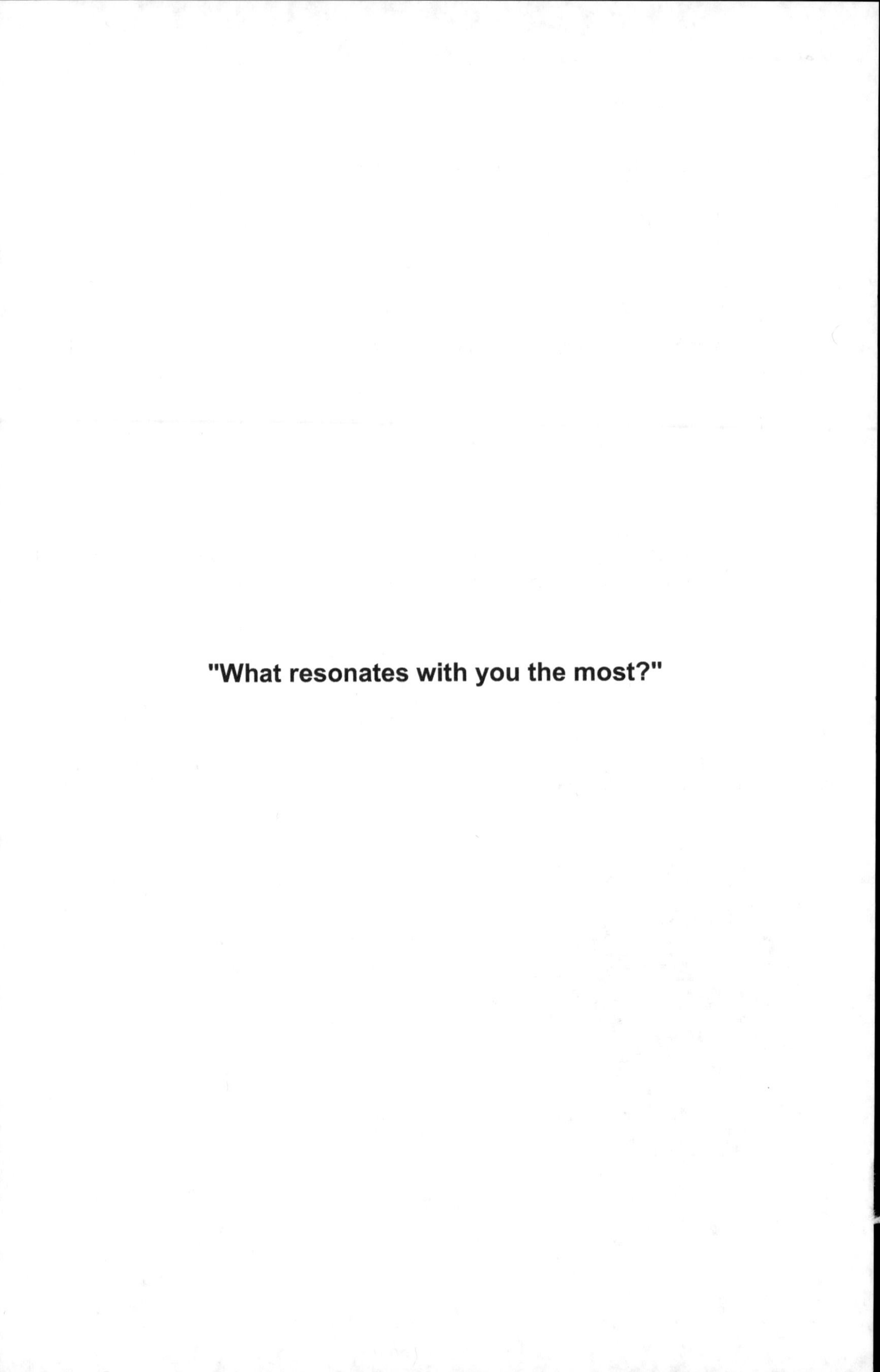

"What resonates with you the most?"

Connection…

"Connection transcends differences; it thrives on the understanding that we are all human."

"In the tapestry of life, it's the threads of our diversity that weave the strongest bonds."

"Every conversation is a chance to discover the threads that connect us, no matter how different."

"We may walk different paths, but the journey of connection brings us closer."

"Finding common ground is the art of recognizing the shared humanity beneath our differences."

Ordelia Jooste

Connection…

"Connection is why we're here; it is what gives purpose and meaning to our lives."
— Brené Brown

"The energy of the mind is the essence of life."
— Aristotle

"We are all different crayons in the box, but when we connect, we create a beautiful picture."
— Unknown

"The most beautiful discovery true friends make is that they can grow separately without growing apart."
— Elisabeth Foley

"What we have once enjoyed we can never lose. All that we love deeply becomes a part of us."
— Helen Keller

Ordelia Jooste

Connection...

"The connection between the hearts of people can make all the difference in the world."
— Unknown

"When we connect with others, we remind ourselves that we are part of something greater than ourselves."
— Unknown

"Ultimately, love is the only thing that matters in life. Without it, we would not exist."
— Leo Buscaglia

"True love is not about perfection; it's about connection."
— Unknown

"The most important thing in communication is hearing what isn't said."
— Peter Drucker

Ordelia Jooste

Connection…

"The way we connect with one another is what defines us as humans."
— Unknown

"The better we feel about ourselves, the more we can give of ourselves."
— John C. Maxwell

"Connection is the energy that is created between people when they feel seen, heard, and valued."
— Brené Brown

"People are much more than a collection of cells and genes; we are deeply interconnected, bound together by the invisible threads of empathy and kindness."
— Unknown

"We're all different crayons in the box, but when we connect, we create a beautiful picture."
*Unknown

Ordelia Jooste

Authenticity…

"Authenticity is the courage to be yourself in a world that often demands conformity."

"To be true to oneself is to honor the unique light you bring to the world."

"In a sea of voices, let your own be heard; authenticity is a powerful statement."

"Rejecting conformity allows us to bloom in our own unique way."

"Your true self is your greatest asset; embrace it unapologetically."

Ordelia Jooste

Authenticity

"Authenticity is the key to unlocking your true potential; don't let the world dim your light."

"Be unapologetically you; the world needs your unique voice to create harmony."

"The path to fulfilment begins with the courage to embrace your true self."

"Authenticity is not a destination; it's a continuous journey of self-discovery."

"In a world that tries to shape you, let your authenticity be the force that shapes the world."

Ordelia Jooste

Authenticity…

"Be yourself; everyone else is already taken."
— Oscar Wilde

"Authenticity is the daily practice of letting go of who we think we're supposed
to be and embracing who we are."
— Brené Brown

"The privilege of a lifetime is to become who you truly are."
— Carl Jung

"To thine own self be true, and it must follow, as the night the day, thou canst not
then be false to any man."
— William Shakespeare

"Don't trade your authenticity for approval."
— Unknown

Ordelia Jooste

Authenticity…

"You were born an original. Don't die a copy."
— John Mason

"Be authentic, be real, and be yourself. The people who matter will love you for who you are."
— Unknown

"The most exhausting thing in life is being insincere."
— Anne Morrow Lindbergh

"When you are authentic, you give others permission to be authentic as well."
— Unknown

"Authenticity is not being afraid of who you are, but being brave enough to let the world see it."
— Unknown

Ordelia Jooste

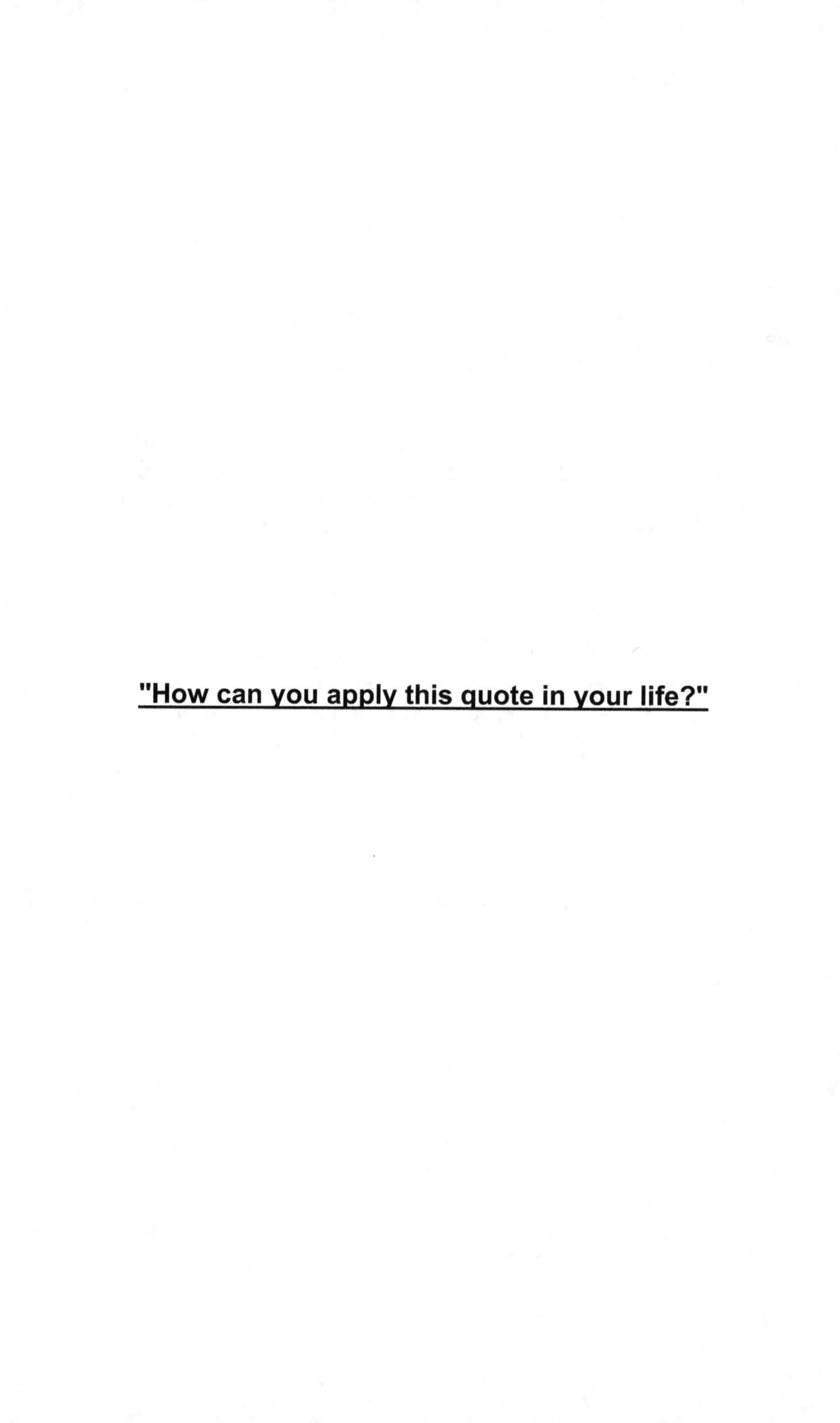

"How can you apply this quote in your life?"

Thank You

Dear Reader,

Thank you from the bottom of my heart for taking the time to explore this book. Whether it was the words, the ideas, or the inspiration you sought, I hope you found something that resonated with you. Your curiosity and willingness to connect with the thoughts and reflections shared here mean the world to me.

In a world that is constantly evolving, moments of pause and reflection are treasures we can hold close. I hope this book has offered you a moment to reflect, to feel, and to connect—whether with yourself, others, or the world around you.

Gratitude for being part of this journey. May you continue to discover, grow, and live authentically.

With heartfelt thanks,
Ordelia Jooste

S – Sensual
U - Unique
N - Natural
F - Feminine
L - Lovely
O - Original
W - Women
E - Elegant
R - Radiant

@sunflowerdiaries – T-shirts for Sale – Proceeds goes to women in distress.